The Kid's Guide to Money

Earning It
Saving It
Spending It
Growing It
Sharing It

Steve Otfinoski

Scholastic

Reference

Scholastic Inc.

NEW YORK   TORONTO   LONDON   AUCKLAND   SYDNEY

Illustrations by Kelly Kennedy
Cover Design by Karen Hudson

Thanks to Matthew Patsky, Victor Laties, John O'Connor, Lynn
Darsh, Kathy Ishizuka, Barry Varela, Adaya Henis, Renee Glaser.

Copyright © 1996 by Scholastic Inc.
All rights reserved. Published by Scholastic Inc.

ISBN 0-590-53853-5

Library of Congress Cataloging-in Publication Data

Otfinoski, Steven.

    Money: earning it, saving it, spending it, growing it, sharing it
/ Steve Otfinoski.
        p. cm. — (The kid's guide to)
    Includes bibliographical references and index.
    ISBN 0-590-53850-0
    1. Children—Finance, Personal. 2. Saving and thrift. I. Title.
II.   Series.
HG179.0786 1996   95-38767
640'. 42'083—dc20   CIP

12 11 10 9   7 6 5 4 3 /0

Printed in the U.S.A.
First Scholastic printing, April 1996

Table of Contents

Introduction
Chapter 1: Earning Your Money

Chapter 2: Spending Your Money

Chapter 3: Banking Your Money

SHOOP

Chapter 4: Sharing Your Money

Chapter 5: Borrowing Money

Chapter 6: Growing Your Money

Appendices:

Introduction

Dollars and Sense–Money and You

Does money burn a hole in your pocket? Or have you saved every dollar you ever received as a birthday present or earned baby-sitting? No matter how much (or how little) money you have now, *The Kid's Guide to Money* can help you take control of the money in your life.

This book has lots of tips for building up your cash supply. But getting and earning money is only half the story. There's a lot to learn about how to spend, save, and share it with others.

In this book, you'll learn how banks can help you save money—a savings account can be a better place to stash your money than a piggy bank. You'll also learn about some things that adults use to help their money grow—such as CDs (not the kind you listen to), mutual funds, and stocks and bonds.

You'll discover ways to get the best value for your money when you spend it, and what to do if you get ripped off. You'll learn why it's sometimes more practical for your parents to write a check or use a credit card than to pay in cash.

You don't have to read this book from cover to cover. Use the Table of Contents at the front and the charts and tables in the Appendices and the Index in the back to look up anything you want to know more about.

The Kid's Guide to Money will help you get some commonsense money sense, starting today!

CHAPTER 1

Earning Your Money

The older you get, the more you are likely to want your own money. To get it, you will have to earn it—either by getting paid for doing chores around the house or by working outside your home.

Your Allowance

An **allowance** is your share of the family income. It's best to get your allowance weekly or every other week. If you get paid once a month or less frequently, you will have to budget your money very carefully to make sure it doesn't run out. But it takes discipline and experience to manage your money.

Your parents may require you to work for your allowance by doing chores. If they do, you might make a contract with them, detailing what you are expected to do each day or week for your allowance. If you don't complete all the required chores, you could agree to forfeit your allowance, or to get less money.

One way to determine your allowance is by using a point system. A certain number of points could be given for each chore, depending on the amount of work and the time required. You could post a list of daily chores on the refrigerator, check them off as they are completed, and then add up the points.

If you earn your allowance, here are some of the chores you might offer to do:

In the Kitchen
- set the table for dinner
- clean up after meals
- take out the trash
- sweep the floor
- make your own breakfast, lunch, and snacks

In Your Room

- pick up your clothes
- put away toys, books, and other belongings
- vacuum the floor
- make your bed

In the Rest of the House

- care for pets (feed, clean up after, walk)
- dust the furniture
- do laundry
- straighten up
- baby-sit for younger brothers and sisters

Outdoors

- rake leaves
- mow the lawn
- shovel snow off walks and driveway

Kid CENTS

"I get five dollars a week for my allowance. I have to do my own laundry, keep my room clean, and sometimes watch my four brothers and sisters while my parents are busy."

—Nicole Lemieux, 6th grade

Working—It's a Great Experience

No matter what kind of allowance you receive, you'll probably spend most of it on things you want and need right away. In order to put aside more money, you may want to supplement your allowance. One way to do this is to work outside your home. But working is not just about earning money. Here are some other benefits you will receive from a job:

Experience
When you work, you learn many important things, such as the value of money, how to do a job well, and how to deal with other people.

Preparation
By trying different kinds of work, you learn what you like to do and what you are good at. This could help you choose a career later. Your work experience will also look good when you apply to college or for a full-time job.

Self-confidence
Earning your own money gives you a sense of accomplishment and independence.

For Someone Else or for Yourself?

You might have a job where you work for someone else—in a store or other business. Then you have a boss who pays you as an employee. However, you'll probably find many more opportunities to work for yourself. This has advantages: You are your own boss and get all the money you earn. You can often work when you want and as much as you want. The disadvantages of working for yourself are that you have to do things by yourself, buy all your supplies, and even motivate yourself. You also have to keep your customers satisfied.

Getting Started in Business

A business is an operation that earns money by providing a service or selling a product. To start your own business you need a few important things: experience, supplies and tools, and advertising.

Here are some businesses you might try:

Jobs That Offer a Service
- shoveling snow
- gardening or taking care of plants
- mowing lawns, raking leaves
- cleaning houses
- taking care of pets (walking, grooming, feeding)
- word processing
- playing records or live music at parties
- baby-sitting

Products You Might Sell
- lemonade and brownies
- old clothes and toys
- homegrown vegetables
- flowers and plants
- handmade jewelry and other crafts
- handmade birthday cards
- gift baskets
- birdhouses

What service or product you decide to offer will depend on your interests and skills. You might start by making a list of things you like to do and things you are good at. Here are some examples:

Interests and skills	Appropriate Jobs
the outdoors	yard work, day-camp helper
young children	baby-sitting
animals	walking neighbors' dogs, taking care of pets while owners are away
computers	office work, teaching people how to operate personal computers
crafts	selling homemade crafts, teaching crafts to others
school subjects	tutoring kids
sports	coaching younger kids

A MONEY MOMENT

According to the Bureau of Labor Statistics, some of the fastest-growing occupations over the next ten years will be chefs, schoolteachers, information clerks, mechanics, gardeners, barbers and cosmetologists, accountants, licensed practical nurses, lawyers and judges, and physicians.

More-Creative Work Ideas

Some of the jobs we've mentioned are ones you have probably thought of yourself. Competition for these jobs may be keen. For example, there may be ten kids in your neighborhood who want a newspaper route but only one paper route available. To earn money, you may need to think creatively and come up with a job that is different.

Here are some suggestions:

- **errand runner:** Run errands for busy people or shut-ins.

- **party organizer:** Organize children's birthday parties, including decorations, entertainment, and maybe even the cake and candles.

- **face painter:** Paint kids' faces at fairs, carnivals, and other special events.

- **toy and electronics assembler:** Put together new products—electronic or mechanical—for people who don't have the time or ability.

- **show organizer:** Put on a show for your friends and neighbors and charge admission. Get your friends to help out, and put on a summer backyard circus, a haunted house for Halloween, or a basement magic show.

Kid CENTS "I sell collectibles, like cards I have doubles of, or if I lend people money, I charge interest."
—Rebecca Weide, 6th grade

The Necessary Experience

Some jobs require more experience than others. Most kids know how to rake leaves or walk a dog, for instance, but making baked goods or giving a dog a bath requires more skill. Where do you get the experience? You might start at home. Baby-sitting for your little brother or sister will give you the experience you need to sit for other people's children. Doing yard work with an older family member will teach you how to clean other people's yards. Your mom or dad might show you how to bake cookies or make lemonade so you can open your own stand.

You might have to learn some jobs from people outside your family. For example, if you're taking over a newspaper route from another kid, he or she will probably show you the route and teach you how to collect money from your customers. To learn to do other jobs—making certain crafts or programming video machines—you may need to look up instructions at the library or at home.

Supplies You Will Need

Some jobs require a few tools. For instance, to shovel snow you'll need a snow shovel. To deliver newspapers you'll need a bag for the papers and maybe a bicycle to get around your route.

Other jobs require more supplies. To clean someone's house you'll need a mop, a broom, and detergent. If you run a refreshment stand, you'll need ingredients, utensils, napkins, and maybe paper cups and plates. If your business is providing music, you'll need a CD or tape player, lots of CDs or tapes, speakers, and, possibly, a portable microphone.

Maybe you have some of the supplies at home or you can borrow them from your parents or friends. Other supplies you will have to buy. Keep track of the money you spend. After you have started your business, subtract the money you have spent from the money you have earned to find your **profit**, the money you made on your business.

Advertising—Getting Out the Word

Letting people know about your business is critical to making it a success. Here are five ways you can advertise:

1. Tell Friends and Family

At family or neighborhood gatherings, tell people about your new business. Offer your service or product for free or at a special discount. If you do a really good job, they might hire you regularly. More important, they will tell their friends and neighbors about your business. Word of mouth can be the best advertising, and it's free. If you make something, such as handcrafted jewelry, give or lend a sample to a friend. When people compliment her on your jewelry, she will send them to you!

2. Distribute Fliers

A flier is a piece of paper that gives important information about your business. A flier should have the following:

- the name of your business
- what service or product you provide
- your name and telephone number
- when you are available
- how much you charge (you may tell people to call you for this information)

You can make your flier by hand or, for a more professional look, design it on a personal computer. Some art will make the flier more appealing. Give your business a catchy name, such as Freddie's Freaky Handmade Jewelry or Julie's Fantastic Yard Work Service. Make plenty of copies on brightly colored paper. To make sure many people see your fliers, distribute them:

- **in your neighborhood:** Slip them in gates or screen doors.
- **on car windshields:** At shopping-mall parking lots or on the street. (For this you'll need permission from the town or other authority.)
- **at local stores or other places of business:** Many stores and community centers have bulletin boards. Be sure you ask the owner or manager for permission to post your flier. Someone may put it up for you, but make sure you bring along tape or thumbtacks in case you have to do it yourself.

3. Go Door-to-Door

If your parents agree that it's safe, this is a good way to let people know about your business. People who have met you are more likely to hire you. To make a good impression, dress neatly and be courteous and cheerful. Leave your flier to remind them that you are available.

4. Advertise in the Media

This form of advertising is probably the most expensive, but it could reap big results. Put an ad in the classified section of your local newspaper or shopper. Keep the ad short and to the point, since you will be charged according to the number of lines of type. Run the ad for several weeks so people will have a good chance of seeing it.

5. Free Publicity

Once you've been in business for a while, you might contact your local newspaper or radio station. If your business is unusual, or if you have been successful, a reporter may want to interview you and even run your picture in the paper.

A MONEY MOMENT Posters and handbills were the first mass advertising. They appeared soon after the invention of movable type in 1440 in Germany.

Deciding What to Charge

What you charge is very important to the success of your business. If you charge too little, you will lose money. If you charge too much, you may not get enough customers. Here are some hints on setting a price:

Check Out the Competition

See what other people are charging for the same service or product. You will want to charge a similar price for your work, or you may decide to charge less and take business away from your competition. If you provide more or better quality products or services, you may charge more than the competition, but be sure you let your customers know your products or services are superior.

Deduct Your Expenses

To make a profit, you have to take in more money from your business than you're spending. If you don't, you'll lose money. Always figure out your expenses when setting a price for work. For example, if you buy brownies at the supermarket for 50 cents apiece and sell them at your lemonade stand for 75 cents to make a quarter in profit, you aren't cheating your customers. The extra quarter is your payment for the time it took to get the brownies and make them available to your customers. If you look around, you might find a discount store where you can buy brownies for less than 50 cents apiece and increase your profit.

Adjust the Price to the Job

If your business provides a service, you may find you have to raise or lower your price to fit the job. For example, one yard you clean may be small, while another may be twice as large. Since the second yard will take more work and time, you should charge the customer more money. In this case, you may consider charging for each hour of your time.

Be Consistent

Once you set a price for a service, don't change it, even if the job takes longer than you expected. If your customers think they are paying one price and you give them a different price when the job is completed, they probably will not use your service again. Better to lose a little on a job than lose a good customer. Learn from your mistake and charge more next time.

Five Tips for Conducting Your Business

The way you conduct your business will determine how many customers come back. Here are the five B's of running a successful business:

1. Be Punctual

If you say you'll show up at a certain time, make sure you're there. If you promise you'll have your product to someone by a certain date, meet that deadline.

2. Be Thorough

Whatever the job, do it well and do it completely. If for some reason you can't finish on time, make sure you return as soon as possible and complete it. Poor or unfinished work may mean you won't get paid.

3. Be Personable

Everyone likes a cheerful worker, so put on your best smile. You'll brighten your customers' days and probably get their business again.

4. Be Accurate

Keep records of each job and each product you sell. Keep track of your customers and what you were paid. You'll need these records to see how much profit you made and if you earned enough money to pay taxes (see page 31). You'll also want to remember your customers so you can offer them your product or service again. Here is a sample work record:

Client	Work Done	Hours Worked	Date	Amount Paid
The Joneses	Baby-sitting	3 hours	6/12	$9.00

Comments: Three kids, one dog, good snacks, asked to clean kitchen.

5. Be Businesslike

Present your client with a bill or receipt. You can make your own bills or buy forms at a stationery store. Keep a copy for your records. If the job is complicated, before you start write a contract or a simple description of the work to be done and the amount you will charge. Getting your customer's signature in advance will prevent any misunderstanding.

Expanding Your Business

When a business is successful, it usually grows. Growth is exciting, but it can also pose problems. If your business grows too quickly without a plan, it may get out of control and fail. It is better to expand slowly and plan each step. Here are some steps to expanding your business:

Take On Employees

Suppose your business is cleaning out people's garages. By yourself, you can't do more than one garage on a Saturday.

But if you hire a friend to help you, you'd probably be able to do the work in half the time and clean out two garages in the same day. Of course, you'd have to pay your helper, but if you double your income, the expense would be worthwhile. As the business owner and manager, you would take a larger share of the profits than you'd pay the people you hire.

Delegate Responsibility

If your business is growing, and you have employees, you may not always work with them. Then you have to delegate—give someone responsibility for doing a whole job. For example, if you have one successful lemonade stand, you might want to open a second. You can't be two places at once, so you could ask a friend to operate the second stand for you. If he or she does a good job, you might even consider making your friend your partner and splitting the profits. Or perhaps your baby-sitting service is growing and you can't keep up with it. You might hire several other kids as baby-sitters while you run the business from your telephone. You'd take the calls for baby-sitting, set up the jobs, and pay your workers an hourly fee. Then you keep the rest of the money as your commission.

Offer More Services or Products

If your lemonade stand is doing well, you might ask your customers what other products they would like. You could add soda or fruit juices. If you keep your stand open in the fall and winter, you might serve hot beverages such as hot cocoa, coffee, and tea.

You can do the same with a service business. If you mow lawns and weed gardens in the summer, think about raking leaves in the fall and shoveling snow in the winter. Make special fliers to remind your customers of your expanding services.

Taxes

Taxes are the monies the federal, state, and city governments collect from residents. Income tax is figured as a percentage of the money people earn. There are also taxes on property, houses, and automobiles, and a sales tax on things you sell and buy. The government uses tax money to pay for many of the services and institutions we enjoy. Taxes pay for schools, libraries, and even hospitals. Taxes also pay for roads, bridges, law enforcement and national defense, and for the national parks and forests you may visit on your family vacation.

Taxes are necessary to run your community, state, and country, but that doesn't mean people like to pay them. Every April 15, the day when most taxes are due, you might hear your parents grumbling. It's no fun turning over hard-earned money to the government, but it's the law, and we all have to do it. Those who don't pay taxes may be fined or even go to prison.

You won't have to pay any income tax unless you earn more than $400 a year in profits in your own business, or $3,800 a year working for someone else. Then you must file a federal income tax form. However, you may want to file an income tax return even if you make less than $3,800 a year as an employee, so that you can receive a refund of the taxes taken out of your paycheck by your employer.

A MONEY MOMENT The average adult worker works from January to May each year just to pay taxes. In other words, about one third of most paychecks goes to local, state, and federal income taxes and Social Security tax.

Social Security

Every month, workers in the United States have a percentage of their salaries taken out of their paychecks by the Social Security Adminstration. It is collected by the Internal Revenue Service, which also collects income tax. The Social Security Administration uses the money to make payments to people who are retired or disabled and to the surviving spouses and children of workers who die.

You must have a Social Security number and card. Employers must require that workers have them, and the Internal Revenue Service requires your parents to list your number when they claim you as a dependent. You also need a Social Security number for financial dealings, such as buying a savings bond.

If you don't have a Social Security number, you, and even your baby brother or sister, can get one. You need your birth certificate and another piece of identification, such as a report card or immunization record. To find out more about getting a number or benefits, your parents can call the Social Security Administration at 1-800-772-1213.

A MONEY MOMENT

The United States was one of the last major industrial nations to set up a social-security system. Congress passed the Social Security Act in 1935, during the Great Depression, when millions of Americans were out of work.

Spending Your Money

So once you've made some money, what do you do with it? You can spend it, save it, invest it, or give it away. In this chapter we'll talk about spending.

Budgeting Your Spending

Spending your money on the things you want may be a lot of fun. But spending has its own set of responsibilities. You have to make sure you don't buy so many things you want that you don't have money for things you need. One way to be sure you have enough money to pay for everything you need is to make a budget. A **budget** is a plan for managing your money on a regular basis. When you follow a budget, you have enough money to meet all your expenses.

Five Steps to Making a Budget

- **Step 1:** Figure out your weekly income, the money you receive from all sources. Count only the money you get regularly, for example, a weekly allowance or money earned from a steady job such as delivering newspapers.
- **Step 2:** Every week, make a list of the things you need to spend money on, such as bus fare, school supplies, and lunches.
- **Step 3:** Make a list of the things you want but could get along without if you had to. These could include going to a movie or buying snacks or a tape.
- **Step 4:** Now list any things that you need to save for.
- **Step 5:** Subtract your needs (the total amount from step 2) from your income. You can spend or save whatever's left. This is your weekly budget.

Here is a sample weekly budget:

Total weekly income: $10.00

NEEDS		WANTS	
lunch/milk tickets	$2.00	snacks at school	$3.00
bus fare (to piano lesson)	$1.50	movie	$3.50
Total needs:	$3.50	**Total wants:**	$6.50
Total weekly income:	$10.00	**Saving for**	
Total weekly needs:	$3.50	**new bike**	$2.00
Money remaining:	$6.50	**Giving donation**	$1.00

Budget notes:

I need to rethink my "want" spending.
I really want to go to the movies this week,
so if I bring my own snacks to school
I can cut that expense and still have
money to save for the bike and make a
donation to charity.

Even if you don't have much of a weekly income, it's still a good idea to create a budget. Managing your money is a habit that's best to develop early in life—starting right now!

Once you plan your budget, it's important to stick to it. Keep track of your spending and budget goals in a notebook. You might want to call it your Money Management Book. Add up each week's total spending. If you managed to keep within your budget that week, you should give yourself a great big pat on the back and 27 hip-hip-hoorays.

Money Jars

Here's one way to make sure you stick to your budget. Take four empty glass or plastic jars and write the following labels on them: NEEDS, OTHER SPENDING, SAVINGS, and GIVING. Put the jars on your dresser or a desk in your room. Every week take your money and split it into the four jars, according to your budget. Take the money out of each jar as you need it.

Advertising—Let the Buyer Beware!

Every day we are bombarded by advertising—on television and radio, in magazines and newspapers, and now even on videocassettes. Advertising can educate and inform consumers about products, but it can influence you to buy things you don't need or can't afford. Advertising can also be misleading and dishonest. Most manufacturers rely on advertising not just to tell people about their products but to persuade consumers to buy them. The more you are aware of the techniques of advertising, the more you will be able to look objectively at a product and make a sensible decision. Here are . . .

Six Ways Advertisers Try to Grab You

1. The Bandwagon Technique

This ad tells you everyone else is buying the product and you'd better get on the bandwagon too, if you don't want to be left out. Don't be motivated by this attempt at peer pressure. Look for a better reason to buy a product. **Example:** Every kid on the block is wearing Snappy Sneakers. Get your pair today and be part of the crowd!

2. The Celebrity Endorsement

A famous person you admire is endorsing this product. If this celebrity uses it, it must be great, right? Not necessarily. Celebrities advertise products because they get paid big bucks by the manufacturer.

Example: Basketball star Jamal Kamal says: "My Snappy Sneakers give me the winning edge on the court. They'll do it for you, too!"

3. The Image-Is-Everything Technique

The advertiser uses pleasing images, music, and fancy camera work to create a favorable impression. In truth, there may be no connection between the images and the product.

Example: In a TV commercial, a pretty girl runs down a country road on a sunny day wearing a pair of Snappy Sneakers. Soft, romantic music plays. As the image fades, a persuasive voice says: "Get back to nature—get a pair of Snappy Sneakers."

4. The Emotional Appeal

This ad also uses persuasive images to get a strong emotion from the viewer. The ad makes you happy, sympathetic, or excited—anything to get you to want to buy the product it's pitching.

Example: A boy is about to make a foul shot in the last seconds of a basketball game. He's the smallest player on either team, and his teammates are looking at him tensely. He looks down at the Snappy Sneakers he's wearing and then up at the hoop.

He throws the ball in the air, and you watch in slow motion as it goes through the hoop, winning the game. The small guy's teammates give a cheer and lift him up on their shoulders. The picture dissolves into the words "Snappy Sneakers— Footwear for Winners."

5. Misleading Claims

This ad makes impossible claims, but does it in such a way that it never actually promises anything. You should be alert to this sneaky technique.

Example: An actor dressed like a doctor is sitting behind a desk with a pair of Snappy Sneakers in front of him. He says, "Wearing the right shoes can correct problem feet." (This may or may not be true, but who says Snappy Sneakers are the right shoe?)

6. The We're-the-Best Technique

This ad leads you to believe its product is better than other brands but doesn't offer any hard evidence.

Example: Four runners are lined up for a footrace. One runner is wearing Snappy Sneakers. The others wear competing brands. The runner in Snappy Sneakers crosses the finish line first. Announcer's Voice: "Snappy

Sneakers leave the competition in the dust every time!"

By now, you're probably convinced you need a pair of Snappy Sneakers. Go to a store and try some on. But if they don't fit—or you like another kind better or if your old sneakers are perfectly good— don't buy them.

Becoming a Smart Consumer

Being a smart spender is a good way to get the most out of the money you have. It's important that you spend your money wisely and make smart choices when you buy.

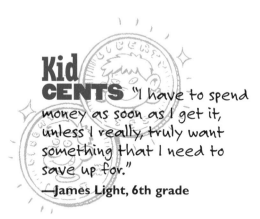

Kid CENTS "I have to spend money as soon as I get it, unless I really, truly want something that I need to save up for."
—James Light, 6th grade

Shopping in Stores

We all shop at stores—department stores, boutiques, music stores, supermarkets. We want to get the most value for our money. To do that you need to think very cleverly. Let's suppose you go to the market to buy some cereal. There are about two hundred different kinds of cereal on the supermarket shelves. Which one is the best value?

Comparison Shopping

One way to find the best buy is to comparison shop. When you shop this way, you compare different brands of a product, whether cereal or laundry detergent. Here are five things to look for when you comparison shop:

- **Price.** How much a product costs is important. A cheaper brand is often just as good as one that's more expensive. In supermarkets, for example, name brands often cost more than store brands, because name manufacturers spend more on promotion and advertising. Actually, the two brands may not be that different. Look for items on sale and discount, too.

- **Size.** Don't be fooled by the size of the package. When you're buying food, look at the weight of the product, which should be listed on the box or container. A smaller box of cereal, for example, might contain the same amount or nearly the same as a larger box of a different brand that costs more.

- **Value.** Food manufacturers are required by law to list the ingredients of their products on each package. If two cereals are the same in price and weight, you might go for the one that has more protein and vitamins and less sugar, fat, and other things that aren't good for you. Similarly, when you shop for school supplies, you may find that there's a large variation of how many pencils or sheets of paper you get in one box or on one pad.

- **Quality.** Examine a product closely to see what it's made of and how well it's made. One brand might cost a little more, but if it's made better, it may be worth the extra money.

- **Premiums.** Premiums are prizes that come with products, especially those that are marketed to kids, such as cereals and snacks. Sometimes the premiums are included in the package. At other times you have to send away for them with box tops, proof-of-purchase codes, or money. You might ask yourself if the premium is worth the extra price of the product. Remember, the premium is a gimmick to get you to buy the product. If you buy a product simply to get a premium, both the premium and the product may disappoint you.

Coupons—A Great Way to Save

Sunday newspapers are filled with money-saving coupons for food, beverages, and other products. Coupons from local stores might come in the mail. Clipping coupons takes time, but it's usually time well spent.

Supermarkets may double the face value of a manufacturer's coupon and sometimes even triple it.

Using coupons regularly at the store can save you and your family hundreds of dollars each year. Just think of what you could do with all that extra money! But don't get carried away with coupons. Be selective. Clip only coupons for products that you really need or want. Buy or make a holder for your coupons so you can categorize them (toiletries, cereals, cookies, etc.) and go through them before every visit to the market. Save the store receipts to keep track of the money you've saved. Put the money saved toward something special.

Buying Expensive Products

Shopping for foods and household items is one thing. Buying something really big, such as a bike or a television set, is another. How do you pick the right one, when a mistake could cost you a lot of money? You should find out

as much as possible about the product
you want to buy and the different
brands available. Here are some tips
for smart buying:

- **Talk to friends and relatives who
  have this product.** Find out if
  they're satisfied with the brands they
  chose, where they got the product,
  and how much they paid for it. If
  they're not satisfied, you need to
  know that too, so you won't make the
  same mistake.
- **Read about the product at the
  library.** Look through back issues of
  Consumer Reports or *Zillions,* the
  young people's edition. These
  magazines will give you information
  about the best values on countless
  products.
- **Check out several stores.** Go
  window shopping before you make
  your purchase. Find out how much
  the same brand costs at several stores.
  You might be surprised how much
  prices can vary on the same item.
  Learn what you can from salespeople,
  but remember that their job is to sell
  as much as they can. Look for
  advertisements for upcoming sales. It
  might be worth waiting a few weeks
  until the item goes on sale.

The Warranty—A Product's Guarantee

Many store-bought products are covered by a warranty. A warranty is a manufacturer's promise to stand behind a product. It tells you exactly what the manufacturer will do to correct a problem you have with the product, within a certain time limit—usually between a year and five years. Some companies include a written warranty with their products, but even if they don't, the law guarantees you an **unwritten warranty**. This means that the manufacturer must guarantee that a product will do what it is supposed to do. If it doesn't, you can demand your money back or an exchange. The only products that are sold "as is," without any warranty, are those that are secondhand or acknowledged to be damaged and so are sold at a big discount.

Some manufacturers include a postcard with each product. Fill it out and send it back to the company immediately to register your warranty. However, even if you don't send in the card, your sales slip with the date of purchase on it should be proof enough of the warranty.

There are two basic warranties:

- A **full warranty** means the product is fully covered for a stated period of time. This means that if it breaks, the manufacturer will pay to have it fixed—including parts and labor.

- A **limited warranty** means that only certain parts of the product are covered under warranty. If other parts break down, the manufacturer is not obliged to repair or replace them. Under a limited warranty parts may be covered, but the customer may still have to pay for labor.

It's a good idea to ask about the details of the warranty before you buy a product. Also find out the location of the nearest service center. If the nearest center is far away, you may want to buy this product from another manufacturer.

Returning a Product to the Store

Whether the product you buy has a written warranty or not, you may return it to the store for a refund or an exchange, usually within 30 days after purchase, for any one of the following reasons:

- it doesn't work right or is broken
- it doesn't fit (clothes)
- it is not what you thought it was
- you changed your mind and no longer want it

Before you return to the store, make sure you bring the following with you:

- the product
- the package it came in
- the sales receipt
- any price tags
- the warranty
- a parent or other adult to help you

When you get to the store, look for the person who sold you the item and state your complaint. Here are some tips on how to make your complaint and get results:

- **Be clear.** Tell the salesperson exactly

what the problem is and why you are returning the product.

- **Be honest.** If the product broke accidentally, say so. Maybe the fact that it broke so easily is reason enough for the store to replace it. Don't lie, even if it means you might not get full satisfaction.
- **Be courteous.** You may be frustrated or even a little angry, but don't show it. The more reasonable and polite you are, the better the chances that the store will be reasonable too.
- **Be firm.** If the person is not responsive, or tells you nothing can be done, stand your ground. If that doesn't work, ask to see the manager or owner of the store.

If a store is reputable, people will try to satisfy you. After all, they don't want to lose a customer. Depending on their policy, they may do one of three things:

- refund your money
- allow you to exchange the product for another product
- give you a store credit for future use.

If you *still* feel you've been treated unfairly, tell the store manager or owner that you are going to report the store to the local Better Business Bureau. This is a nonprofit corporation that protects the public from unfair advertising and business methods. At this point the owner may refund your money rather than get into trouble with the Better Business Bureau. If he or she still refuses to cooperate, report the store. Look in the local Yellow Pages for the nearest Better Business Bureau, or write the Council of Better Business Bureaus Incorporated for a list. Its address is in the appendix on page 112.

A MONEY
MOMENT
There are Better Business Bureaus in over two hundred cities in North America. Each year these bureaus received more than six million calls for information and assistance.

Shopping on the Street

Street vendors often sell great things at lower prices than you can get in stores. But before you shell out your hard-earned cash for a cheap pair of designer jeans or a new wristwatch, make sure it's exactly what you want. When you buy from a store, you can bring the product back if there is some problem. Return to the corner the next day and the vendor may well be gone. Though many street vendors are honest businesspeople trying to earn a living (remember your lemonade stand), there are two types to beware of:

- **Those selling counterfeit name brands.** What you think is a name brand may very likely be counterfeit—fake or illegally copied goods. If you look closely, you might find shoddy material and workmanship. The name brand on the label may even be different. In other words, this isn't the brand you think it is, and the vendor has gotten around the law by changing the name by a letter or two. Most people won't even notice the difference until they get home.
- **Those selling stolen goods.** If a deal seems too good to be true, it probably is. If someone offers you fancy jewelry or a fancy watch or camera for little money, it may be stolen. Beware.

Shopping Through the Mail
Buying things through mail-order companies can be fun and more

convenient than shopping in stores. But you should be careful whom you buy from and what they're selling. Here are some helpful hints to keep in mind when you order anything through the mail:

Look for Facts

Don't be fooled by fancy ads. Many products in magazine ads and mail-order catalogues look bigger and better than they really are. Look for dimensions, materials, and other descriptive facts about the product. If there aren't any, that might tell you this product isn't worth buying.

Read the Entire Ad

Most mail-order houses charge postage and handling in addition to the price of the product. But they may try to hide these charges in small print. Read the ad carefully so you know what you're paying for and how long the delivery time will be. Also, music clubs often make tempting introductory offers of free tapes or CDs. However, once you join the club, you are obligated to buy more, often at inflated prices. Read the fine print first!

Check Your Order

It's easy to make a mistake when filling out an order form. You could put down the wrong order code and get the wrong product. Or you could neglect to add postage and handling charges and delay receiving your purchase. Double-check your order or have an adult look it over.

Never Send Cash
Bills and change can get lost or stolen in the mail. Always send a money order or have your parents write a check. A canceled check is proof that you paid for the product.

Keep Good Records
Save the ad and the address of the company. If your order never arrives or isn't what you expected, write to the mail-order company. If the ad appeared in a magazine, also write to the magazine's editor or publisher. If you still don't get satisfaction, call your local post office. They'll put you in touch with the nearest postal inspector who handles illegal use of the mail. You may or may not get your money back, but by reporting the fraud you could help to stop this company from ripping off others.

Unordered Merchandise
Sometimes you may get something in

the mail you didn't order. It might be a tape or CD from a music company or a selection of postage stamps from a hobby company. You are asked to consider buying the product or send it back.

Sending people merchandise they didn't ask for is illegal. You do not have to send back such merchandise or pay for it. If you do decide to send it back, simply write "return to sender" on the outside of the package and put it in the mail. As long as you haven't opened the package, you will not have to pay for return postage.

Shopping by Television

Most TV cable systems carry at least one shopping channel, where viewers can see merchandise and order it by calling a toll-free number. Many other TV stations run "infomercials," half-hour-long commercials, often starring celebrities, to sell products and services such as beauty aids and diet programs. These stations and programs have become tremendously popular.

Because it is so convenient, television shopping leads many people to buy things they don't really need. Often viewers are further pressured to buy by announcers who claim the product is being offered for a limited time or is quickly running out of stock. Be careful of shopping by television. Sometimes the merchandise is not what you expected and is more expensive that what you would pay in a store. Make sure you have your parents' permission before ordering a product over the telephone.

A MONEY MOMENT

TV shopping has become a major business since its debut in 1985. Jewelry is the most popular merchandise, and the typical viewer/shopper is a working woman. An interactive system is being tested that will allow shoppers to view products three-dimensionally and even rotate packages using remote control to read ingredients and other information.

Tipping

Tipping is giving money to someone who provides you with a service. The tip is a bonus for doing a good job. Often, the person makes a low wage and depends on the tips for part of his or her income.

Here are some people you should tip:

- restaurant waiters
- taxi drivers
- barbers or hairstylists
- hotel bellhops who help carry your luggage to your room
- housekeepers in hotels

In most cases, your parents or another adult will pay the tip. But there may be a time, such as when you're eating in a restaurant with your friends, when it's your turn to tip.

How Much Should I Tip?

The standard tip for waiters, barbers, and cab drivers is 15 percent of your bill, before the tax is added. But what you actually give should depend on the kind of service you receive. If the service is poor, you should leave a smaller tip. If the service was exceptionally good, you should leave a larger tip.

Working Out the Tip

Here's an easy way of calculating your 15 percent tip:

- **Step 1:** Take 10 percent of the bill. To do this, you simply move the decimal point one place to the left. For example, if the bill for your meal came to $7.00 before tax, 10 percent would be $0.70 or 70 cents.

- **Step 2:** Take half of the 10 percent. This is 5 percent of your bill. Half of 70 cents, for example, would be 35 cents.

- **Step 3:** Add the two figures together to get 15 percent: $0.70 + $0.35 = $1.05. This is a 15 percent tip for a $7 bill.

JOE'S COFFEE SHOP

RECEIPT

blueberry pancakes	$3.25
w/bacon	.50
eggs special w/ham	2.75
milk	.50
Subtotal:	$7.00
7% tax:	.49
total:	7.49
Thank you!	

Banking Your Money

So you're earning money and spending it wisely and well. If your budget is very tight and you don't have much left over, you can keep it in a safe place at home. But if you can save money, even a little bit at a time, things get more fun . . . and also more complicated.

Why Save?

Spending is all very well, but if you want something you can't afford right away, the best way to get it is to save for it. Saving money also means you'll have it when you need it—in an emergency, such as when your bicycle needs repairs. Finally, there are things in life—college, a car, a house—that are so expensive that you'll never receive the whole cost at one time. The only way you can pay for them is to save and perhaps borrow some money to add to your savings.

Kid CENTS "I save about one half of my money, so if I see something I like I have money to buy it."
—**Kate Roche, 5th grade**

Two Kinds of Saving

There are two kinds of savings you can consider when managing your money:

- **Short-term savings** is just what it sounds like—money you save for a short time to buy something you'll need soon.
- **Long-term savings** is money you save

longer for bigger, more expensive things, such as a new bike, a school trip, or even college. This money can be held in a savings account or a certificate of deposit (CD) at a bank. (see pages 63 and 79.)

A MONEY MOMENT

The first coin money was made in the kingdom of Lydia, now Turkey, about 640 B.C. The coins were made of gold and silver and were stamped with a lion's head, the symbol of the Lydian king. Paper money was first developed in A.D. 1300 by the Chinese, because they didn't have enough metal to make coins.

Banks—A Good Place to Keep Your Money

A bank is a business that accepts deposits of money and makes loans. Most banks offer many other services to customers.

Four Reasons to Put Your Money in a Bank

1. Banks Are Safe

If you put money in a bank, you can get it back. All banks are insured.

2. Banks Make Your Money Grow

In exchange for allowing the bank to lend your money to other customers, most banks pay you money, called interest.

3. Banks Offer Helpful Services

You probably won't be able to use most of these financial services now, but you will when you're a little older. These include investment programs, loans, special savings plans, and automated teller machines (ATMs).

4. Banks Make It Harder for You to Get Your Money

If you keep your savings at home, you might be tempted to spend some or all of them. When your money is in a bank, you'll think twice before spending it.

A MONEY MOMENT Ever wonder where piggy banks come from? In England in the 1400s there were two meanings for the word "pig," or *pygg*, as it was usually spelled back then. One meaning was a baby hog and the other was a piece of crockery, a container made of clay. Somehow those two meanings have come together in those cute clay pigs we keep our pennies in.

The Savings Account

The best way to start saving is to open a savings account at a bank. Most banks won't let kids open their own accounts, so you probably will have to open a **savings account** with a parent or guardian. This means the account is opened in your name and the adults. While you may deposit money by yourself, your parent or guardian must sign for you when you want to take out money.

Many schools offer students the opportunity to open a savings account with a local bank. Students can put money into their savings accounts on a designated banking day held every week or two at school. Find out if your school has a banking program. If it doesn't, see if you can help start one.

A MONEY MOMENT

The first banks were introduced by the Babylonians about 4,000 years ago. Modern banks began in Italy in the 1500s. Italian bankers attracted borrowers by laying out their money on benches in the street. The word "bank" comes from the Italian *banco*, which means bench.

Depositing and Withdrawing

Each time you make a **deposit** and put money into your account, or make a **withdrawal** and take money out of your account, you must fill out a slip of paper showing the transaction. Most banks give you deposit slips when you open an account, but they also supply their counters with blank deposit and withdrawal slips. To put money into your account or remove it, you must fill out a form. You write in your name, the date, the total amount of money you are adding or removing, and your account number. A withdrawal slip looks much the same except for its label. Here's what a deposit slip looks like:

National National Bank USA		NNB USA

Savings Deposit

SAVINGS DEPOSIT

CREDIT THE ACCOUNT OF (*Your name*)	DATE
Daniel Otfinoski	8/2

This deposit is subject to the applicable savings account Rules and Regulations of National National Bank USA
Please endorse all checks and write your account number on the back of each check.
All checks are accepted subject to collection.

Cash	5 50
Checks	25 00
List each check separately	

ENTER YOUR ACCOUNT NUMBER
▼
ACCOUNT NUMBER

ENTER YOUR TOTAL DEPOSIT
▼
TOTAL AMOUNT

1 1 2 3 5 8 1 3 2 $ 3 0 5 0

⑊5000740 3⑊

Kinds of Savings Accounts

There are different kinds of savings accounts. One of them is the **passbook** account. A passbook is a bank book that shows you how much money you have in your account. Here is what a page in a passbook looks like:

ACCT. NO. 03-4751-6225

	DATE	WITHDRAWAL	DEPOSIT	INTEREST	BALANCE	TELLER
1	8/25		+20.00		20.00	ℋm
2	9/18		7.00		27.00	Nf
3	10/30		12.00	.02	39.02	an
4						
5						
6						

When you deposit or withdraw money, you give your deposit or withdrawal slip to the bank **teller,** who receives and gives out money, and show your passbook. The teller will record the addition or subtraction and your new balance, the total amount in your account. Your passbook shows you exactly how much money you have in your savings account.

As banks become increasingly computerized, many of them have done away with passbooks. Most offer **statement savings accounts.** Usually you can make a withdrawal or deposit with a teller or at an automatic teller machine (ATM) (see pages 74-77). With this kind of savings account, you receive a written record of your banking in the mail every month. A savings account statement will look like this:

STATEMENT OF ACCOUNT PERIOD 03/07/96 - 04/04/96					
SAVINGS	BEGINNING BALANCE	DEPOSITS, OTHER CREDITS	WITHDRAWS, OTHER DEBITS	INTEREST PAID	ENDING BALANCE

DEBITS AND CREDITS			
DATE	DEBITS(-)	CREDITS(+)	DESCRIPTION

Interest—Why It Pays to Save

When you keep your money in a piggy bank, it doesn't earn any more money. Put in a dollar and you get out a dollar. But when you open a savings account, your money starts to grow every day with **interest**—a percentage of the balance in your account that the bank pays you to use your money. The bank uses your money and that of other depositors to make loans to other customers. When it lends your money to someone else, it charges that customer interest. This interest is a higher percentage than the rate paid to you. For example, a bank might pay 3 percent interest on savings accounts and offer loans at 7 percent interest.

Interest is computed in two ways:

Simple Interest

A bank paying simple interest pays you a certain percentage of every dollar you save. Say you have $1,000 in the bank. This is your **principal,** the total amount you deposit in your account. The bank pays you 3 percent annual interest. That means you get 3 cents on every dollar every year. At the end of a year you will have earned $30 in simple interest on your $1,000.

Compound Interest

Most banks calculate compound interest, and it's a little more complicated. Every day the bank calculates that day's interest and adds that interest to the principal in your account. So every day the bank pays you interest not only on the money you originally put in the account but also on the interest the principal has already earned. If the bank is paying you 3 percent annual interest, you'd make $30.45 in compound interest on your $1,000 the first year. That may not seem like much more than simple interest, but every penny you can put into your account earns compound interest, and your savings will grow over time. Over long periods of time, the difference between simple and compound interest can be significant.

Not all interest is compounded daily. Some banks compound the interest monthly, quarterly (every three months), or semiannually (every six months). This must be clearly explained in its advertising.

Here's an example of how your savings build with compound interest. Imagine that when you were eight, you deposited $1,000 in the bank at the annual interest rate of 3 percent compounded daily, and just left it there until you graduated high school at the age of 18. If interest rates remained the same, your $1,000 would have grown to $1,349.84—all thanks to compound interest!

Some banks have a minimum amount they will accept in a savings account without charging a fee, and the percentage of interest banks pay their customers varies, so it's best to shop around before opening a savings account.

The Checking Account

A checking account is another kind of bank account. It's for money you want to spend. You need quite a bit of money for a checking account (you might ask at a few banks just how much), but if you have a business, it can come in handy. You can draw money out of a checking account to buy things or pay bills by simply writing a check. Checks are a safe, easy, and convenient substitute for cash.

If someone gives you a check, you must endorse the check in order to deposit or cash it. Turn the check over and write your name across the top end of the check. But don't endorse the check until just before you cash or deposit it because once it's endorsed anyone can cash it.

Opening a Checking Account

As a young person, you probably can't open your own checking account. Most banks require that a person opening a checking account be 18 years old and have a full-time job. You may be able to open a checking account with a parent or guardian. Every time you write a check, the adult must cosign it.

When you open a checking account, the bank gives you a checkbook containing checks with your name and address on them. Every time you write a check, you record the amount in your checkbook register, a kind of record book, and subtract it from your balance. Depending on how much money is in your account, a bank may either charge you a per-check or monthly service fee (because it considers the balance small) or pay you interest (because you have so much money, it wants to encourage you to keep it in that bank).

Here is what a check looks like filled out:

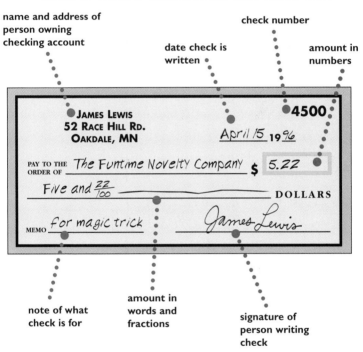

Here's how you would record the check in your checkbook:

NUMBER	DATE	DESCRIPTION OF TRANSACTION	PAYMENT/DEBT	√T	DEPOSIT/CREDIT	BALANCE
						25.00
4500	4/15	The Funtime Novelty Company	5. 22			5.22
		for magic trick				19.78

new balance

Here's how you endorse a check:

For deposit only to
checking account
#5 5467 4566 7654

James Lewis

Here are some tips on writing checks:

- **Make sure you have enough money in your account to cover the check.** If you don't, you will be overdrawn and the bank may not honor the check. You'll be charged a fee.

- **Always write in ink.** This way no one can erase or change the amount of money on your check.

- **Draw a line to fill out the money line.** This way no one can add to the amount you've written. (See sample check on p. 71.)
- **Don't forget to sign your name.** The check is worthless without your signature.

Kid CENTS

Should kids be able to have their own checking accounts? Here are two different views:

"Yes, because then we wouldn't have to bother our parents for money, and we wouldn't have to carry a lot of money."
—**Chika Anekwe, 5th grade**

"I'm not sure that kids should have checking accounts. If I had checks, I'd use them all the time and probably run out of money."
—**Jodi McLaughlin, 5th grade**

The Travels of a Check

Suppose you write a $10 check to the grocery store to pay for lemons, sugar, and cups for your lemonade stand. Here's what happens to the check.

- **Step 1:** The store manager takes your check, along with the other cash and checks the store received that day, to the bank.

- **Step 2:** The bank stamps your check on the back to show that it's been received and can't be used again.
- **Step 3:** The bank sends it to a clearinghouse.
- **Step 4:** The clearinghouse instructs your bank to subtract $10 from your account and instructs the store's bank to add $10 to the store's account.

The whole thing happens without any physical paper money moving at all.

A MONEY
MOMENT High-speed electronic machines can process about 100,000 checks in an hour. The machines are programmed to "read" sorting instructions written in magnetic ink on the bottom of each check.

Automated Teller Machines— Instant Money!

An easy way to get money from your bank account is with an **automated teller machine** (ATM). An ATM is a mechanized teller that is open when the bank is closed, usually 24 hours a day. ATM machines are located in bank lobbies and other convenient locations.

You've probably been with your parents when they've used an ATM to get some money. The customer puts a small plastic card issued by the bank into a slot and pushes a number code on a set of buttons. This series of numbers is called a **personal identification number** (PIN). Having a secret code keeps your money safe. No one can get into your account without your card and your PIN.

After you press the numbers of your code, the ATM screen will ask what kind of transaction you want to make. At most ATMs you can withdraw money, make deposits, check your balance, transfer money from one account to another, and even pay bills. Then the machine returns the ATM card and gives you a receipt showing what you just did.

Some people use ATMS even when the bank is open because it's quicker than going to a teller. However, some banks charge a fee every time a customer uses an ATM, so watch out.

A MONEY MOMENT

Among modern, industrialized nations, people who live in the United States save the least money. According to one survey, U.S. households save only 4.1 percent of their **disposable** income, the money available to spend, compared with 9.2 percent in Great Britain, 13.1 percent in France, and 15.3 percent in Japan.

If you use an ATM, you should be careful to follow these safety rules:

- **Guard your PIN.** When using the ATM, look around to see that no one is watching you, and complete your business as quickly as possible.
- **Avoid unsafe ATMs.** Thieves sometimes hang around ATMs waiting

for people leaving with cash. Don't use an ATM in a high-crime area or on the street in an unprotected area. Also, try to use ATMs during daylight hours. Most robberies occur at night.

Other Services Banks Provide

Safe-Deposit Boxes

These fireproof boxes are locked in big vaults and rented to customers. They're the perfect place to keep valuables such as jewelry, rare coins, important papers, or maybe even your comic-book collection.

Special Checks

If you don't have a checking account and need a check, banks can provide you with one-time certified checks, cashier's checks, registered checks, or money orders. These are often better than a personal check because the bank guarantees them. If you don't have an account, the bank will charge you a fee.

Traveler's Checks

Traveler's checks are also guaranteed by a bank or a separate company and are often used by people on vacation who don't want to carry a lot of cash. Even if you don't have a checking account, your parents may be able to buy traveler's checks for you to use.

When the check is purchased, you sign your name in the upper left corner. Then, when you are ready to use the check, you sign your name in the lower right corner. The person cashing the check will look to make sure the two signatures match and may even ask for another piece of identification with a signature. Traveler's checks usually come in

multiples of $10—$10, $20, $50, $100. If you cash one, you will get change as if you had spent money. For example, if you give a $20 traveler's check for a purchase of $15.95, you will receive $4.05 in change. Banks usually charge fees for traveler's checks when you purchase them, but some other organizations provide them free to customers.

Other Special Accounts

- **Trust accounts:** money put aside for one person by another, such as a grandparent for a grandchild.

- **Certificates of Deposit** (CDs): money deposited for a specific amount of time for which the bank pays a higher rate of interest than on regular savings accounts.

- **Individual Retirement Accounts** (IRAs): savings people put away for when they are no longer working. The interest earned on these accounts is not taxed until the person is retired and begins withdrawing the money.

- **Loans:** Banks lend money to people to help them buy cars or houses or to start businesses. The bank charges interest for these loans. (More about borrowing money in chapter 5.)

Banking by Computer

Banks, like other businesses, are computerized. In some areas, bank customers can now pay bills, transfer money from one account to another, and see if a check has cleared using a personal computer at home, work, or school. Direct deposits, in which a person's paycheck is automatically deposited into his or her account, are also done by computer.

Whether you open a savings account or a checking account at a bank or keep your money in a piggy bank at home, saving money is important. It means you will have money when you need it most!

Sharing Your Money and Your Time

Giving your money to others may not be something you think of doing. After all, it's your money, so why shouldn't you spend it all on yourself?

Donating money is a good thing to do because it helps . . .

- **people** who are less fortunate than you are, including those who are ill or unable to provide for things they really need;

- **you** to be a responsible person who is concerned about problems and injustices in the world;
- **the world** to become a better place to live in. If everyone shared what they had, there would be less suffering.

Giving Money

Many people, adults and kids alike, don't give or give less than they could. Here are four common excuses:

1. My parents give. So why should I?

It's important for every family member to give something. No matter how much your parents give, your contribution is important. And perhaps you'll want to choose different causes from those your parents support.

2. Everybody's looking for a handout these days. I can't give to them all, so I won't give to any of them.

No one can give to all the worthy causes in the world, and it's very difficult to decide what to do. But if you give to the charities you believe in most or those closest to home, you'll be all right.

3. I don't have much money to give. How can my nickel or dime make a difference?

It doesn't matter how little or how much

*you give. Every little bit helps, and if
you save it up from week to week, you
can give a single, larger donation.*

**4. I don't trust charities. I think
they're just ripping us off.**
*Of course a few charities are phony,
but there are laws to help keep them
honest. Before you give your money to
any organization, you can check it out
with your state's attorney general's
office. If the group isn't legitimate, the
attorney general's office should know.*

How Do I Give?

There are two main ways to share your
money:

- Make a monthly or annual donation to
  a favorite charity, to your place of
  worship, or to a person running for
  public office who wants to do things
  that you want done.
- Give your loose change to recognized
  charities, such as the Salvation Army, or
  local charities that put jars on public
  counters.

How Much Should I Give?

This is a question only you can answer.
The amount you give depends on what
you can afford, what needs exist in your
community, and how much you want to
give. It's important, however, that you try

to give some money on a regular basis. That way, giving becomes a part of your money management. Come up with a figure you feel comfortable with and build it into your budget, along with saving and spending. You could even set aside your donations using the money jars mentioned in chapter 2 (see page 38).

Some people give as much as 10 percent of their total income to charity each year. You may want to start lower, but let's use this percentage as an example. Say you get, from all sources, $10 each week. You decide to give 10 percent of that to charity. That's $1. If you divide it among several causes, you may want to let the money add up before you send in your donations.

If you should get an increase in your allowance, a sudden spurt in your earnings, or a generous gift from a relative, you may want to make a larger, one-time donation. You've had some good luck, so why not share it with others?

Kid CENTS "I make church donations and give to a national AIDS foundation and groups against animal cruelty."
—**Thomas Ivers, 6th grade**

Giving in Other Ways

This book is about money, but you can give in other ways.

Things

You may have lots of things you no longer want or need that other people could use. These include old clothes, toys, books, and eyeglasses. You also might have bottles, old newspapers, and other recyclables lying around that you can cash in and then give the money to a needy cause.

Groups such as Goodwill Industries, the Salvation Army, and the Red Cross often have receptacles where these items can be dropped off. Before holidays, they hold toy drives. Some organizations will even come to your house to pick up donations.

A MONEY MOMENT The Red Cross is named for its distinctive flag, which resembles the flag of Switzerland, where the organization was founded in 1863. In Muslim countries a red crescent, a Muslim religious symbol, replaces the Christian cross on the flag, and the organization is called the Red Crescent.

It's a Tax Deduction!

If you earn your own money by working either for other people or for yourself (see page 31), you may have to pay taxes. If you give money or things to a charity, you can deduct the value of the donation on your income tax return. However, if you drop off your giveaways in a bin, you'll have a harder time proving your deduction. So go to a Goodwill center or other charitable store with your items, and get a receipt. It's an important record for tax purposes.

Your Time—Be a Volunteer

Someone once said "Time is money." And it's true. By giving your time, you are giving someone else a valuable resource and giving yourself a rewarding experience.

Here are a few ways you can help:

- Visit someone who's in the hospital.
- Help prepare sandwiches for the homeless or hungry at a shelter.
- Volunteer as a helper at a hospital or health-care center.
- Read to a person with poor eyesight.
- Organize a group to visit a convalescent home and entertain the patients with songs and music.
- Help out a neighbor who has a baby.
- Tutor a younger student.

Raising Money for a Good Cause . . . Your Own

There will be times when you give your time, money, and possessions to a group or organization of which you are a member. Here are some examples:

- Your Scout troop or 4-H chapter wants to go on a camping trip.
- Your school band is invited to perform in a parade out of town.
- Your youth group wants to make a long-distance trip to work on a service project.

These are worthy projects, but they all take lots of money for travel, food, and lodging. Here are some ways you could raise the funds:

- Hold a car wash.
- Give a bake sale.
- Put on a talent show.

- Collect newspapers, cans, and deposit bottles for recycling.

You might think of ways to tie in seasonal events and holidays into your money-raising activities. Try one of these:
- Make and sell wreaths and sell Christmas trees for the holidays.
- Prepare and sell sandwiches, snacks, and desserts on Super Bowl Sunday.
- Sell flowers for Mother's Day or homemade cards for Valentine's Day.

One East Coast youth group raised money for a service project in Appalachia by selling "shares" in the project. Shares were really a way to let people sponsor the trip. Shareholders were invited to a thank-you dinner and slide show on the group's return.

Giving your money and your time can be as much fun as spending your money on yourself, and sometimes even more satisfying.

Borrowing Money

There may be times when you want something and can't wait until you earn or save enough money to buy it. It might be a new bike or a television set for your room. Or, in the case of your parents, it might be a new car or even a house. One way to get the money you need is to borrow it.

Where Do You Go to Borrow Money?

A Friend or Relative

This can be the best way to borrow money. People who know you are most likely to lend you money. They also probably won't charge you any interest. And they might be flexible about when they get their money back.

A Bank

Lending money to people is one of the services banks provide. As a young person, you can't get a bank loan. But you might be able to when you grow up. To get a bank loan, people have to show they have a regular job and can pay back the money, plus interest. Sometimes they also have to show they have something of value—a house, a car, or other property—called **collateral**, that could be used to pay off the loan if they can't pay back the money.

A Finance Company

Finance companies lend money too. They often charge higher interest on loans than banks do. But some people can't get a loan from a bank because they don't have enough collateral or a good-enough employment record. They have to use finance companies even though they're more expensive than banks.

A Credit Union

Credit unions are privately run financial institutions that benefit their members. They work like banks, lending money that members deposit with them. Many credit unions are formed in workplaces and in small communities and offer loans at a very low rate of interest.

A MONEY **MOMENT** Alphonse Desjundins set up the first credit union in North America in Quebec, Canada, in 1900, and in 1908 he helped set up the first one in the United States in Manchester, New Hampshire.

Who Can Borrow Money?

A person's ability to borrow money is directly related to his or her credit rating. The word "credit" comes from the Latin *creditus,* meaning "trust." You may trust a friend to pay you back the money she borrows because you know her, but banks and other financial institutions have to be more businesslike about it. They evaluate people's credit on the basis of their . . .

- **income**—how much money they earn;
- **job history**—their ability to hold a job and their present employment;
- **credit history**—their record for paying bills on time.

If a person is considered to be financially reliable, he or she will receive a good credit rating and the bank will probably lend him or her money. People with a record of paying bills late or not at all receive poor credit ratings and have trouble getting loans.

Kid CENTS Should kids have their own credit cards? Here are two opposing views:

"Yes, because I think we kids are capable of handling money. Grown-ups just don't trust us. It's sad really."
—Thomas Ivers, 6th grade

"No, because things would get out of hand and they would owe a lot of money."
—Nick Rising, 6th grade

Credit Cards—Paying With Plastic

A **credit card** is a small piece of plastic that identifies you as a customer in good standing of a credit company. It allows you to buy merchandise and services up to a limit the bank sets on that card.

Here's what a credit card looks like:

When you use your card, you are giving the credit company permission to pay the merchant and to charge you. At the end of each month, the credit company sends you a statement showing all the purchases you made on your card in that time period. You are usually given 25 days or so to pay your bill. If you don't pay off the entire balance, you will have to pay interest on the rest of the money you owe. Sometimes you'll pay interest on your purchase as well. Most credit companies require that you pay a minimum amount of your bill each month, but a few require you to pay the whole balance.

There are more than 7,000 credit cards available to consumers. Most of them fall into two main categories:

Major Credit Cards

These are national or international companies that offer their cards through a bank, another financial organization, or a large business. Some of the best-known major cards are Master Card, Visa, American Express, Discover, and Diner's Club. These credit cards are accepted by thousands of businesses, stores, and restaurants in the United States and around the world.

Business-Specific Credit Cards

These credit cards are issued by individual businesses such as department stores and oil companies. They can be used only to buy from branches of the store or from gas stations operated by the oil company.

How do credit cards make money for the companies that issue them? They charge interest on unpaid balances and many charge their customers annual fees. In addition, the businesses that accept these credit cards pay a small fee to the company.

Choosing a Credit Card

Although you are too young to get a credit card on your own credit rating, here is some useful information to tuck away for the future:

Pick a Card You Will Use

Some people have dozens of credit cards and don't use many of them. Or they use them all and spend more money than they should. Choose cards you will use and keep only a few cards. This way you won't be tempted to spend lots of money and won't be paying lots of annual fees and interest.

Read the Small Print

Read the contract before you sign up for a credit card. For example, some companies charge you interest from the date of purchase and have no grace period to pay off your balance. That's no bargain! Other cards, such as American Express, require you to pay off the balance every month or suffer a penalty. Some companies charge an annual fee and others don't. Some have higher rates of interest than others. Check out the facts and then make your decision based on them.

Look for Extras

Find a credit card that offers a bonus. Some cards award points toward the purchases of products. One card company gives points toward the purchase of a new automobile. One large video rental business offers a major credit card that allows you to build up points toward free video rentals. And some cards donate to charity a percentage of the amount you charge. But watch out—some of these companies have higher annual fees or higher interest rates.

Three Golden Rules of Using a Credit Card

Many people can't handle credit cards. They run up big bills and then pay the minimum each month. They end up paying walloping interest fees, and they never pay their cards off completely. Here are three golden rules to follow that will help you to use credit cards responsibly:

- **Rule #1:** Don't buy on impulse. When you shop with a credit card, no money exchanges hands, and it's easy to forget how much you're spending. When you shop, have a list of things you need and stick to it. Pay attention to the prices and keep track of the total. It will all have to be paid off.

- **Rule #2:** Pay off your bill each month. The interest most credit card companies charge is very high—as high as 20 percent. If you carry your balance from month to month, the interest will add up quickly. If you can't pay off the bill right away, your debt will continue to grow. If you discipline yourself to pay off your balance each month, you'll save yourself a lot of money.

- **Rule #3:** Stay within your credit limit. Every credit card has a limit on the credit you can use. If you go over that limit, you will pay a penalty or possibly have your card privileges suspended. To avoid this, keep track of what you spend on your card each month.

QUICK CREDIT CARD COMPANY
ACCOUNT NUMBER 3425-5368-7245
PAYMENT DUE DATE: 8/16   MINIMUM PAYMENT DUE: $32

STATEMENT DATE:	TOTAL CREDIT AVAILABLE:	NEW BALANCE:
8/1	$436.00	$64.00

TRANSACTIONS:

PAYMENTS AND CREDITS

JULY 13	PAYMENT—THANK YOU	−$85.00

PURCHASES

JULY 5	FRANK'S PIZZA	$12.00
JULY 12	PAULA'S PET SHOP	$15.00
JULY 24	COOL CLOTHES FOR COOLER KIDS	$37.00

	TOTAL PURCHASES	$64.00

Big-Time Borrowing—Mortgages

A **mortgage** is a loan from a bank or some other financial institution used to buy a house or a piece of land. The borrower pays back the mortgage in monthly installments over a period of time, often as long as 30 years. Part of each payment goes to pay off the balance of the loan, called the **principal**, and part goes to pay off the interest on the loan. If the borrower fails to make regular payments, the lender can **foreclose,** or stop the mortgage and take over the property or home.

A MONEY MOMENT

The word "mortgage" comes from the Latin-derived words *mort*, meaning dead, and *gage*, meaning pledge.
A mortgage was originally a pledge you made to the death.

CHAPTER 6

Growing Your Money

Another way to make your money work for you is to invest it. Investing is buying something in the belief that it will grow in value. It might be a rare baseball card, a government bond, or a share of stock. The value of your investment can increase more rapidly than the money you keep in a bank savings account. It may also lose value just as fast. Investing money, unlike saving money, involves a certain risk.

Turning a Hobby Into an Investment

A **collectible** can be any object that you buy and can then sell to someone else for a profit. You may already own some collectibles. They include:

- baseball or other trading cards
- postage stamps
- comic books
- coins
- dolls
- old records.

It is not enough, however, simply to collect these things. You must know which are valuable and which are not. Here are some tips on collectibles:

- **Become knowledgeable.** Learn everything you can about what you're collecting. Join a collectors' club, attend shows and trade fairs. Read books and price guides that will give you up-to-date information on what your collectibles are worth.
- **Look in unlikely places.** If you buy collectibles from dealers, you will probably pay top dollar for them. Shop at tag sales, flea markets, and junk stores. You might find a prize collectible amid a lot of junk and for

very little money. This is part of the fun of collecting.

- **Keep records.** Keep an inventory of your collection, including the price paid for each item and what you sold or traded it for.
- **Keep your collection in good condition.** Collectibles lose much of their value if they are in poor condition. When they are good as new, or in **mint condition,** they are worth the most. Protect your investment. Keep your valuable comic books in plastic bags, your coins in containers or mounted in cellophane, and your trading cards in albums.

More than many other investments, collectibles are fun to own. Consider your collection a hobby first and an investment second. If you can make money with your collection, that's great. But you should enjoy collecting for itself, too. Any collectible is only worth what someone else is willing to pay for it, and dealers will always pay you less for a collectible than they will sell it for. That's how they make a profit. If you start investing in collectibles simply to make money, you may end up disappointed.

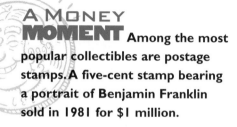

Buying Savings Bonds

You might already have some government savings bonds. Maybe your uncle or grandmother gave you one for a birthday or at holiday time. He or she went to the bank and bought the savings bond in your name. The bank charged half the face value of the bond. When the bond matures, you can cash it in at the bank for the face value. When your uncle bought that savings bond, he was lending the government money. The extra money you get when you cash in the bond is the interest the government pays to use your uncle's money.

Here is what a savings bond looks like:

Here are two tips for taking care of your savings bonds:

- **Put them in a safe place.** Keep them in an envelope in a bureau drawer or, better yet, let your parents put them with other important family papers.

- **Keep records.** Write down the serial number of your bond and the date on which it matures (ten years for series EE bonds). Keep this information in a safe place too. You want to remind yourself when your bond matures, so you can redeem it.

Stocks and the Stock Market

Businesses need money to grow. To get this money, some businesses sell **shares**, units of ownership in their company. These shares in a company or business are called **stocks**. A person who buys one or more shares of stock is a **stockholder**. If there are one hundred stock shares in a company and you own them all, you own the entire company.

Most big companies have hundreds, sometimes thousands, of stockholders. The stockholders pay a certain price for each share, as little as a dollar and as much as about a thousand dollars. Since the value of a company's shares goes up and down, stockholders hope to buy low and sell high. That is, if the share price goes up, stockholders can sell their shares for more than they paid for them and make a profit. If the share price goes down, however, and a stockholder sells, he or she will lose money. If a company should fail, its stockholders can lose their entire investment. That's where the risk comes in.

Kids can buy stocks just like anyone else. Many companies will sell you one share of stock. And some companies pay their stockholders **dividends**—a share of the company's profits—so you can make money from your investment even if you don't sell.

And you can take your dividends and buy more stock with them. That way you can invest more and more.

Buying and selling does cost money, though. You have to pay a **broker** to do the actual buying and selling for you.

Choosing a Company to Buy Stock In

When deciding to buy stock, you should look for . . .

- **A company that interests you and produces something that you like.** It might be video games, athletic footwear, clothes, or music. This way, you're helping a company you approve of, and you're more likely to stay interested in your investment.

- **A company that makes money and has potential to grow.** This may sound like an obvious choice, but until you investigate different companies, you may not know which will provide the best return on your investment. Write the company for its **annual report.** It will tell you how much the company made in the year just past and in previous years. You may need an adult to help you understand the annual report.

- **A company that is socially responsible.** Many people believe it's important to invest only in companies that care about people and the environment. Find out if a company is environmentally sound and whether it respects human-rights issues wherever it is invested in the world. (See page 118 for a book that will help you.)

You may have heard people say they "play the stock market," because the excitement of picking stocks and watching them go up and down is like a game. But they're playing with real money. One safe way to learn about the stock market is to "play" without actually owning stock. Some students form teams at school, and the teacher gives them an imaginary amount of money to invest. They follow their stocks in the paper or by dialing a stock-quote phone number, just like real stockholders. The team or school that ends up with the most money from their investments is the winner.

"I think it's really neat how you could invest $50 in a company and in a couple of weeks have $300. It was like money was growing on trees."

—**Matthew Hull, 6th grade, on playing the stock-market game in school**

Mutual Funds—Another Way to Play the Market

If all this sounds too complicated for a kid, it's often too much for adults, too! That's why many people invest in **mutual funds.** Mutual funds typically consist of a group of stocks, bonds, or money-market securities from more than one source. (For more about bonds, see pages 109-110.) The company that sells the mutual funds hires financial experts to select the stocks or bonds for its customers. When you buy shares in a mutual fund, you are buying a pool of stocks or bonds from several select companies.

Because the money in mutual funds is spread around, your risk is lower than with a single stock. If some companies do poorly, others may do well. You also save money because many mutual funds are **no-load.** That means you pay no commission or extra fee for buying into the fund. Management fees, however, may run $10 or more a year.

There are three basic kinds of mutual funds:

- **income funds.** These funds are for investors who need the money they invest to live on. They usually pay high dividends, grow slowly, and are considered low risk.
- **growth funds.** These funds usually pay low dividends or none at all, grow more quickly, and are often a higher risk. They work best for investors who can leave their money in the fund so that their investment can grow over a long period of time.
- **balanced funds.** These funds combine income and growth stocks and bonds.

While you are young, you should think about putting some of your money into growth funds. Although they may rise and fall over a number of years, they probably will make more money than safer, but lower-interest, income funds.

A MONEY MOMENT

Two of the most colorful stock-market terms are **bull** and **bear.** A bull market is one in which stock prices are rising. A bear market is one in which prices are falling. Some people believe the terms originated from the fighting style of these two animals. Bulls attack upward with their horns, while bears sweep down on an enemy with their paws.

Bonds

Bonds are another way that corporations can raise money to build and grow. Like savings bonds, corporate bonds are not shares in a company, but a loan. The company issues a bond certificate that promises to pay back the loan in a certain time period, along with interest at a set rate. When you buy most bonds, you know exactly what you are getting. When the date of payment, or **maturity,** arrives, you can redeem your certificate for cash.

Businesses aren't the only organizations that sell bonds. City, state, and the federal governments need money to build and grow too. They use the money raised from bonds to build such things as roads, bridges, schools, libraries, and hospitals.

Bonds offer a number of advantages over stocks. Here are a few of them:

- **Most bonds are low risk.** The safest bonds are issued by the United States government. Your money is guaranteed. But most other bonds are very safe too. In most cases, even if a company fails, its bondholders will get their money back. This seldom happens to stockholders.

- **Some bonds are tax free.** You don't have to pay state or local income tax on most government bonds. You don't have to pay federal tax until you cash in the bond. If the bond is spent on college tuition and your family income is low enough, you won't have to pay any federal tax.

- **Many bonds can be bought directly.** You can buy bonds at most banks.

Keeping Track of Your Investments—Reading the Financial Pages

When you invest in stocks or mutual funds, or just track them to learn more about investing, it's a good idea to check their prices regularly. You can find information about how stocks, bonds, and mutual funds are doing in the business section of your daily newspaper. This section also contains articles about new businesses, which industries are growing and which are not, and successful businesspeople. All this information can be useful to you.

Stock and mutual-fund prices are usually listed at the back of the business section of your newspaper. The first time you look at these pages, with their long columns of tiny numbers, you might well be confused. But with a little practice, you can find the information you want. (See pp 114-116.)

Appendices

• • • • • • • • • • • • • • • • • • • •

Resource Lists

Consumer Protection and Education Organizations

To complain about products, write:

Correspondence Branch
Room 692
Federal Trade Commission
6th Street and Pennsylvania Avenue
Washington, DC 20580

Office of Consumer Affairs
Department of Commerce
Room 5718
Washington, DC 20230

To report mail fraud, speak to your local postal inspector or postmaster, or write:

Chief Postal Inspector
United States Postal Service
Washington, DC 20260-2100

Consumer Advocate
United States Postal Service
Room 5910
Washington, DC 20260-6720

To report hazardous products or an injury from using a hazardous product, write or call:

Product Safety Hotline
United States Consumer
Product Safety Commission
Washington, DC 20207
1-800-638-2772

To get a list of the nearest Better Business Bureaus, write:

Council of Better Business Bureaus, Inc.
4200 Wilson Boulevard
Arlington, VA 22203

To learn about the social responsibility of a company, write or call:

The Council on Economic Priorities
30 Irving Place
New York, NY 10003
1-800-729-4237

Selected Volunteer Organizations

American Red Cross
Programs & Services
Department
17th & D Streets NW
Washington, DC   20006

Boys Club of America
771 First Avenue
New York, NY   10017

Children's Action for Animals
American Humane Education
Society
350 South Huntington Avenue
Boston, MA   02130

4-H Youth Development
Extension Service
U.S. Department of Agriculture
Washington, DC   20250

Girl Scouts of America
830 Third Avenue
New York, NY   10022

Harvest of Hope
Society of St. Andrew
P.O. Box 329
State Route 615
Big Island, VA   24526

Junior Achievement
45 Club House Drive
Colorado Springs, CO   80906

Keep America Beautiful
99 Park Avenue
New York, NY   10016

National Wildlife Federation
1412 16th Street NW
Washington, DC   20036-2266

Special Olympics International
1350 New York Avenue NW
Suite 500
Washington, DC   20005

UNICEF
333 East 38th Street
New York, NY   10016

How to Read Stock Tables

At the back of the business section of your newspaper, you will find a group of enormous charts in tiny print. If you want to get information about stocks, look at the charts labeled New York Stock Exchange, American Stock Exchange, and NASDAQ. Each line of those charts tells how one company's stock did on the previous business day. Look at the bottom of the page for an example.

Terms defined

- **52-week high and low:** The highest and lowest price a share of that particular stock has sold for in the last year, but not including the previous day. YardInc has had a pretty big range of prices, from $8 to $18.37. (Prices are listed in fractions instead of in the decimal cents that you're used to.) Shares of stock are bought and sold for whatever the seller and buyer agree on. That price changes from day to day, even from minute to minute.

- **Stock:** The abbreviated name of the company. These are

Stocks

52-week		Stock	Dividend	Yield	P/E
				%	ratio
high	low				
$18\frac{3}{8}$	8	YardInc	.08	0.8	25
27	$22\frac{3}{4}$	Lemo	1.72	6.5	10

pretend companies called Yardwork Inc. and Lemonade Stand.

● **Dividend:** The amount of money paid in a year to each shareholder on each share he or she owns. YardInc pays 8¢ per share. If you owned 100 shares, you would be paid $8 per year on your stock worth $1,062, or 0.8%. On the other hand, Lemo pays $1.72 per share. If you owned 100 shares, you'd receive $172 per year on your stock worth $2,637, or 6.5%. A company that is using its profits to grow (building new factories or buying other companies, for example) doesn't pay out much to its stockholders in dividends. An older, slower-growing company pays more.

● **Yield %:** The dividend expressed as a percentage of the stock price. For example, for Lemo, $1.72 (the dividend) is 6.5% (the yield) of $26.37 (the last price of the day).

● **P/E** (price/earnings ratio): The price of a share at the closing of the stock market that day (find it under **Last**) divided by the company's earnings (profit) for the past year. If a company—for example, YardInc—has a price/earnings ratio of 25, that means you could buy 1 share of stock for 25 times the amount the company

Sales 100s	High	Low	Last	Change
69	11	$10\frac{1}{2}$	$10\frac{5}{8}$	-1/4
7650	$26\frac{5}{8}$	$26\frac{1}{4}$	$26\frac{3}{8}$	-1/8

earned per share during the last year. Lemo has a price/earnings ratio of 10. That means you'd have to pay 10 times the company's annual earnings per share to buy a share of that stock. The P/E ratio indirectly tells you the earnings per share. Just divide the price by the ratio. Lemo earned approximately $2.64 per share last year and paid out more than half its earning in dividends ($1.72).

If a company has a high price/earnings ratio (above 20), it usually means that it is a young, fast-growing company. If a stock has a low P/E ratio, it usually means that it is a low-growth or mature company.

- **Sales 100s:** The number of shares of that stock sold that day, figured in batches of 100 shares. Add two zeros to find the actual number of shares. So, 6,900 shares of YardInc and 765,000 shares of Lemo changed hands on this day.
- **High:** The highest price a share of this stock sold for in the course of the day.
- **Low:** The lowest price a share of this stock sold for in the course of the day.
- **Last:** The last price a share of this stock sold for in the course of the day.
- **Change:** The difference between the last price this day and the last price the day before.

For Further Reading

Saving Your Money

Adler, David A. *Banks: Where the Money Is.* New York: Franklin Watts, 1985.

Dunnan, Nancy. *Banking.* Morristown, NJ: Silver Burdett, 1990.

Spending Your Money

Berry, Joy. *Every Kid's Guide to Intelligent Spending.* Chicago: Children's Press, 1988.

Council on Economic Priorities. *Shopping for a Better World.* San Fransisco: Sierra Club, 1994.

Schmitt, Lois. *Smart Spending.* New York: Charles Scribner's Sons, 1989.

Giving Your Money and Volunteering

Henderson, Kathy. *What Would We Do Without You?: A Guide to Volunteer Activities for Kids.* White Hall, VA: Betterway Publications, 1990.

Earning Your Money

Amazing Life Games Company. *Good Cents: Every Kid's Guide to Making Money.* Boston: Houghton Mifflin Company, 1974.

McDiarmid, Teena. *Making Money.* Milwaukee: Penworthy Publishing, 1988.

Borrowing Money

Kane, Elmer R. *How Money and Credit Help Us.* Chicago: Benefic Press, 1966.

Investing Your Money

Faber, Doris. *Wall Street: A Story of Fortunes and Finance.* New York, Harper & Row, 1979.

The Conscientious Investor's Guide to Socially Responsible Mutual and Money Market Funds and Investment Services. New York: Interfaith Center on Corporate Responsibility, 1993.

Young, Robin R. *The Stock Market.* Minneapolis: Lerner Publications, 1991.

Glossary

allowance—a regular portion of money given to members of a family.

annual report—a document that public corporations are required by law to file each year describing the company's business, income, profits, and losses.

assets—what a person or company owns—property, money, and investments.

automated teller machine (ATM)—a computerized terminal at which customers can perform a variety of banking transactions, 24 hours a day.

balance—the amount of money in a bank or other financial account.

bank—a business that accepts deposits of money and makes loans.

bear—a person who believes that prices on the stock market are about to go down.

bear market—the stock market when prices of shares are going down.

bond—1. an investment in the form of a loan, which is repaid with interest by a business or the government. 2. the paper certificate that proves the purchase of a bond.

broker—an agent who buys and sells for a client. *See* stockbroker.

budget—a written plan for managing money on a regular basis.

bull—person who believes that prices on the stock market are about to go up.

bull market—the stock market when prices of shares are going up.

business—an operation that earns money by providing a service or selling a product.

certificate of deposit (CD)—an investment in which money is deposited for a specific amount of time at a specific rate of interest.

check—a printed form that the holder of a checking account can fill out and use to pay others without using cash.

checking account—a bank account from which the customer can withdraw money by writing checks.

collateral—a valuable possession, such as a house, that is held as a guarantee that a customer will pay back a loan and that the financial institution can sell if the loan isn't repaid.

collectible—an object of value, such as coins or rare comic books, that can be collected and traded or sold to someone else for a profit.

credit card—a small plastic card that identifies a person as a customer in good standing of a credit company and allows him or her to buy merchandise or services on credit.

credit line—an amount of money, approved in advance, that a customer can borrow from a bank or some other financial institution.

credit rating—a measure of whether a particular person is reliable when it comes to paying back loans.

credit union—a privately run financial institution that lends money to its members, often at low interest rates.

currency—paper money in circulation in a particular place.

deposit—an amount of money put into an account.

disposable income—the portion of a person's budget available for nonessential spending.

dividend—a payout per share of a company's profits that it divides among stockholders per share.

finance company—a business that lends money, usually at higher rates than banks do.

foreclose—to take over a property or home on which the owner has failed to make regular mortgage payments. The lender can then sell the property to recover the amount of the loan.

growth fund—a mutual fund that is based on stocks with a high potential for growth.

income—the total sum of money received from all sources.

income fund—a mutual fund that is invested in order to pay a steady return at low risk.

income tax—a tax that federal, state, or city governments collect from residents based on the money they earn.

individual retirement account (IRA)—a savings or investment account in which a person deposits money to be withdrawn when he or she is no longer working.

infomercials—elaborate half-hour-long television commercials, often featuring celebrities, for various products and services, such as beauty aids and diet programs.

interest—money paid for the use of someone else's money.

Internal Revenue Service (IRS)—the government agency responsible for collecting federal taxes.

investment—something, such as stocks, bonds, or collectibles, in which a person invests money, time, or effort in the expectation that it will increase in value.

maturity—in banking, the time when a bond can be sold for its face value.

minimum balance—the amount of money a person must have in a bank account to keep it active or to avoid paying a penalty or monthly fee.

mint—in new or like-new condition.

mortgage—a loan from a bank or other financial institution used to buy a house or other piece of property.

mutual fund—a group of stocks or bonds, managed together, in which people can invest money.

no-load fund—a mutual fund that doesn't charge a commission for buying or selling shares.

overdrawn—having written checks for more money than is in a checking account.

passbook—a savings-account book in which the teller records the balance, deposits, withdrawals, and interest.

personal identification number (PIN)—a secret number a customer uses to access his or her bank account through an automated teller machine.

premium—a prize or incentive offered with the purchase of a product.

principal—the original sum of money owed or invested.

profit—the amount earned by a business after expenses are met.

safe-deposit box—a fireproof box located in a bank vault that can be rented for the storage of valuable possessions.

savings account—a bank account to which a person makes deposits and accumulates interest with the objective of saving money rather than spending it.

share—a unit of ownership of the stock of a company.

Social Security—a fund managed by the government to which workers contribute through taxes and which pays benefits to people who are retired or disabled, or who are survivors of a deceased worker.

statement account—a bank account in which the person

receives a printed monthly record of deposits, withdrawals, interests, penalties, and service charges.

stock—the fund of money a company raises by selling shares to investors.

stockbroker—a professional buyer and seller of shares of stock who charges clients a fee for services.

stockholder—a person who buys one or more shares of a company's stock.

taxes—the money that governments collect from residents.

teller—employee in a bank who handles customer transactions, which include receiving deposits and cashing checks.

tipping—giving money to someone, such as a waiter, who provides a service.

traveler's checks—checks for fixed amounts guaranteed by a bank or financial institution that are often used instead of cash.

unwritten warranty—a guarantee, protected by law, that says all new merchandise, except that which is heavily discounted, must do what it is supposed to do, or the merchant is obliged to fix or replace it.

Wall Street—the financial district and center of the stock market in New York City.

warranty—a promise from a manufacturer to stand behind a product. A full warranty covers all parts and labor. A limited warranty covers only certain parts.

withdrawal—an amount of money taken out of a bank account.

Index